A CHILD'S HISTORY OF LONDON

Written by Nicholas Whines

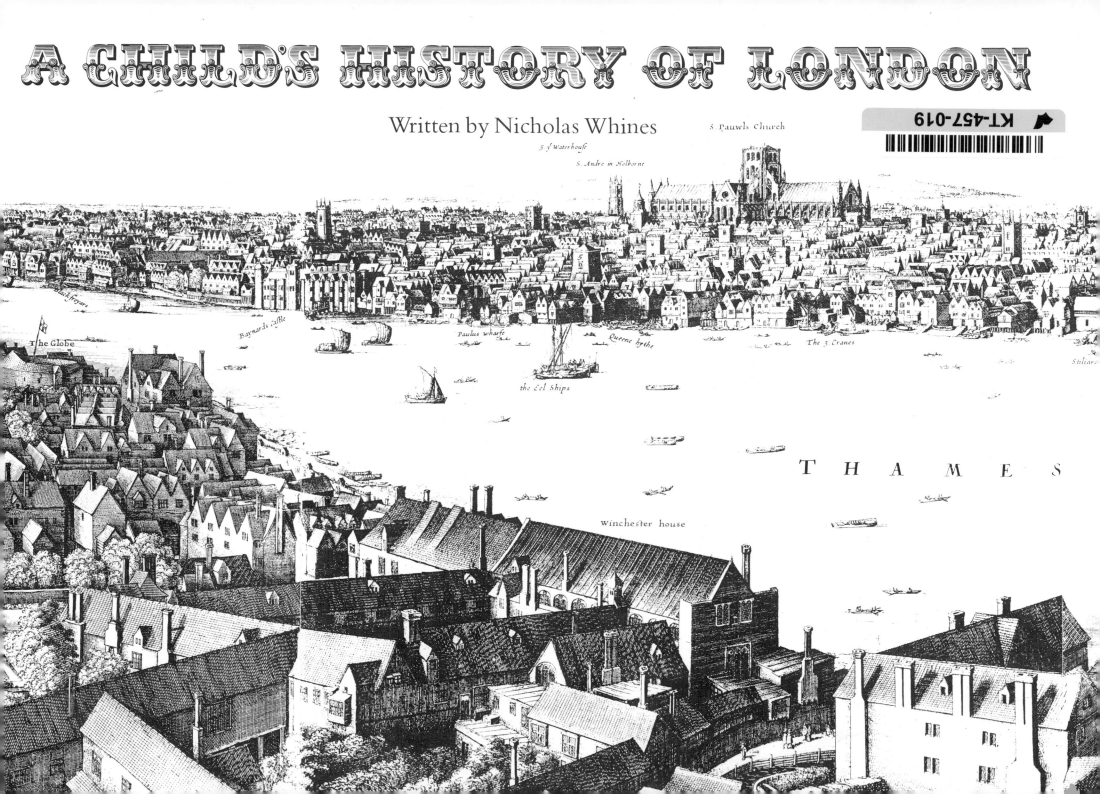

S. Pauwls Church

S. y Waterhouse

S. Andre in Holborne

Blackfryars

Baynards castle

Paulus wharfe

Queene hythe

The Globe

the Eel Ships

The 3. Cranes

Stiliar

Winchester house

T H A M E S

TOWER HILL 1842

THE TOWER AND MINT.
FROM GREAT TOWER HILL

If you visited the *Tower of London* about 140 years ago this is the view you would have seen.

Can you see some children playing marbles? A carter leads his horse. A group of horsedrawn cabs wait to be hired. They probably do good business bringing tourists to see London's most famous building, the Tower of London. On the extreme right we can see the rigging of ships on the river Thames moored along *Tower Wharf*. Three sailors walk by. One staggers under a huge bundle. Goodness knows what he is carrying.

Our view-point is *Tower Hill* just to the north-west of the Tower itself. In previous centuries this was a place of execution. Huge crowds would gather to watch people die. But this afternoon all is peace and sunlight.

The artist who drew this picture was called Thomas Shotter Boys. He has included himself in the foreground. Can you see him? Over the last 500 years many artists have drawn and painted pictures of London. In this book you will find a small selection of their work. Their pictures help us to answer two questions. What did London and Londoners look like in the past and how did the city grow?

Not all the artists painted in the same way. Some were more accurate. Some included more detail. Some changed the perspective to fit everything in. Some left out things they thought upsetting. Some were not interested in just recording a scene: they drew their pictures to tell a story, or make a point, the way a cartoonist does. Some artists never even visited London but drew from other people's pictures.

Nevertheless these pictures contain a great deal of evidence about the past for you to look at. So examine all the pictures carefully. Look at all the detail and see if you can answer some of the questions contained in the captions. Can you spot a line of washing and a boy with a hoop?

LONDON TODAY

This is London today. The London which we know. You can't see all of it. In fact you can only see a small fraction of it. This is the business centre of London which is sometimes called the City.

In the photograph you can see some of London's most famous buildings. We are looking west. Directly below is *St Katharine's Dock*.

① One of the newest buildings is the *National Westminster Tower*. This was completed in 1980 and is 600 feet (182m) high. 2,500 people work inside the building.

② This is *London Bridge*. Notice it isn't falling down. Well it shouldn't because it was only completed in 1973. There has been a bridge here spanning the river Thames for nearly 2,000 years.

③ This is *Tower Bridge*. Don't confuse it with London Bridge. Tower Bridge was built in 1894 in the days of Queen Victoria.

④ *St Paul's Cathedral* is more than 250 years old. Its splendid dome still stands out well even though today it is surrounded by larger, modern buildings.

⑤ This is the oldest building in the photograph, the *White Tower*. It is the central keep of the Tower of London. The White Tower was built by the Normans about 1078.

To follow this book you should start by examining the map on the opposite page which shows you the location of some of the famous buildings you will be looking at. The illustrations are arranged in chronological order and help to tell the story of the history of London.

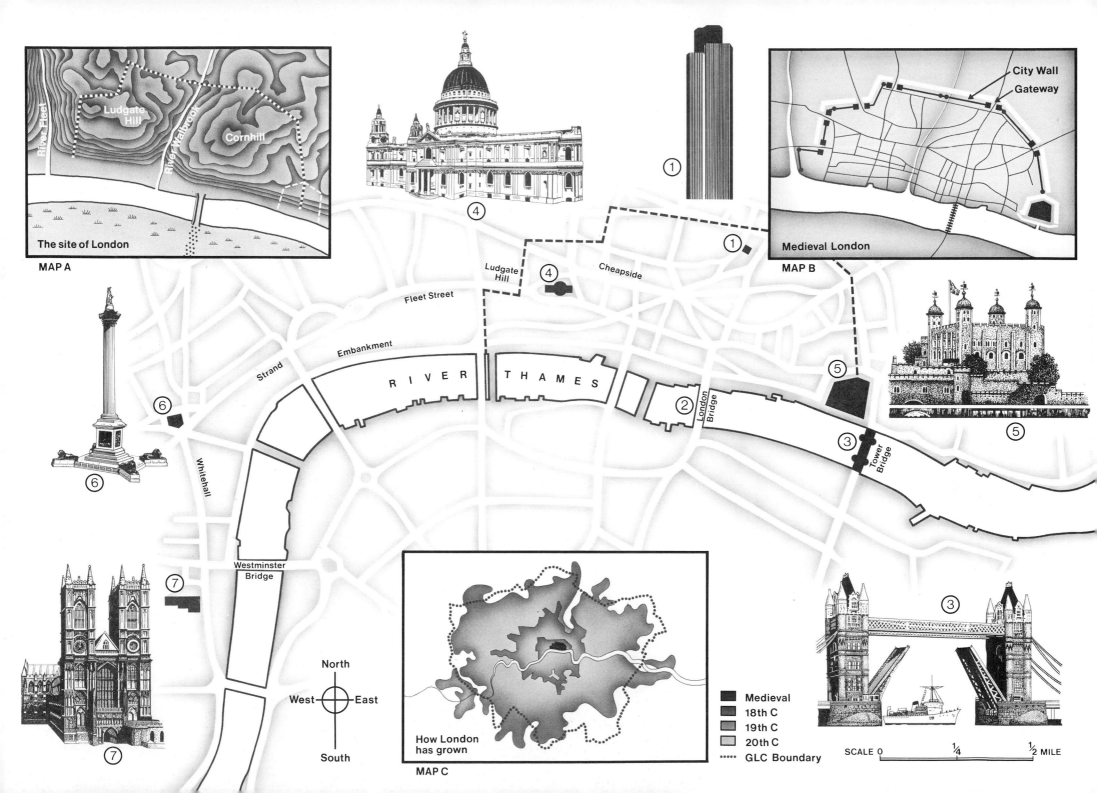

MAP A

River Fleet

Ludgate Hill

River Walbrook

Cornhill

The site of London

MAP B

City Wall

Gateway

Medieval London

① ④ ⑤

Ludgate Hill

Cheapside

Fleet Street

Embankment

Strand

R I V E R   T H A M E S

London Bridge

②

③

Tower Bridge

Whitehall

⑥

Westminster Bridge

⑦

North

West — East

South

MAP C

How London has grown

Medieval
18th C
19th C
20th C
GLC Boundary

SCALE 0   ¼   ½ MILE

THE ROMAN CITY

London was founded by invading Romans in the first century AD and called Londinium. One of the first things they must have done when they reached the Thames was to build a bridge. To start with they might have lashed a number of boats together. Later they must have built a wooden bridge.

Just to the north of the bridge stood two low gravelly hills. Just right for building a camp to defend the bridge. South of the river a gravelly bank amid the marshes provided a firm foundation for approach roads.

The Romans were famous for their roads which they built to move their armies rapidly around the country. Bridges attract roads and

soon London Bridge was the centre of a whole network of communications. The river Thames itself provided a quick and easy way of reaching Europe and the rest of the Roman Empire. Traders and merchants soon arrived to sell their goods and before long London had become a busy port.

London in the Third Century

① In the centre of the bridge a section lifts up to allow ships with masts to move up river.
② In the top corner of the city lies the Army Fort.
③ A massive wall runs all the way round the city. Sections of the wall still exist although these have been greatly repaired over 1800 years.

◄◄ The medal shows a citizen of London welcoming a Roman ruler. You can see a galley on the river and a gateway. No other views of Roman London survive.
◄ This is an artist's impression of the site of London before the Romans came. Notice the two rivers running into the Thames: the *Fleet* and the *Walbrook*.

The illustration opposite is also a ► modern artist's reconstruction based on archaeological evidence. It shows Roman London in the third century.

④ Along the wall were fortified gateways where roads entered the city. The Roman wall and its gateways roughly define the area we call the City of London. (See map B on page 5.)

⑤ In the Basilica worked the city officials. In front of it lies the Forum, the main market and meeting place. Around the forum would have been a whole variety of shops and workshops.

Medieval London

In the year 410 AD the period of Roman rule finally came to an end. The Roman cities of Britain were told by the Emperor they had to defend themselves as best they could.

We know little of the history of London over the next 600 years. Saxon invaders came and settled. For a while London declined then flourished again. The Vikings came and on one occasion London was burnt and its citizens were slaughtered. But once again the city was rebuilt. By 1000 AD London was the largest city in the land.

In 1042 AD Edward the Confessor became king. Edward was a particularly religious man. He built *Westminster Abbey* about two miles upstream from the old Roman city. He died a few days after his new church had been completed.

In this picture from the Bayeux Tapestry we catch a first glimpse of London. How accurate it is we cannot tell. No other pictures of London from this period still survive. It is very likely that the English women who stitched the Tapestry had never been to London.

Notice the man on the left who is just about to fix the weathercock. This shows how new the building is. On the right the body of the old king is being carried from his palace to the Abbey for burial.

On the death of Edward the Confessor, Earl Harold became King. It was Harold who was defeated and killed by William of Normandy at the Battle of Hastings in 1066. The Bayeux Tapestry tells the story of William's victory in the form of a strip cartoon.

Westminster Abbey was one point around which London developed. The other was the old walled city and port left behind by the Romans.

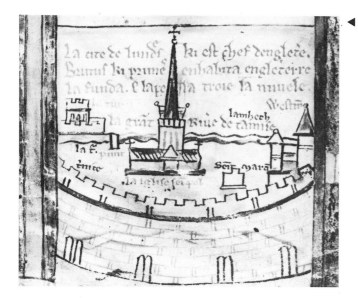

This is the earliest view of the City of London so far discovered. It is dated about 1252 AD, nearly 200 years after the Norman invasion. On the left it shows Westminster Abbey. In the centre is old St Paul's Cathedral. On the right is the Tower of London. Two wavy lines indicate the river Thames. In the foreground is the wall with its battlements and gateways.

▼ The view below comes from a medieval book of psalms. It was called Constantinople by the monk who drew it. But it seems likely that it is really a view of London. One clue is the weathercock on the top of St Paul's Cathedral. Notice the signs on poles outside the various buildings. In a time when few people could read, signs were very important in helping people find their way about.

A man called William Fitzstephen lived in London during the 12th century and wrote one of the first descriptions to have survived of London and its citizens:

During the holydays in summer the young men exercise themselves in the sports of leaping, archery, wrestling, stone-throwing, slinging javelins beyond a mark, and also fighting with bucklers (shields) ... the maidens dance beneath the uprisen moon.

When the marsh beyond the walls to the north of the city freezes over, the young men go out in crowds to divert themselves upon the ice. ... They bind under their feet the shinbones of some animals and taking in their hands poles shod with iron they are carried along with as great rapidity as a bird flying or a bolt discharged from a crossbow.

◄ London about 1500

This painting was made in about 1500 to accompany a book of poems written by a Frenchman called Charles Duke of Orleans. Charles had been captured at the battle of Agincourt in 1415 and held to ransom in the Tower of London. Because nobody paid the ransom, he was kept a prisoner for 25 years. The painting tells his story.

At the bottom you can see Charles arriving at the Tower by way of the river gate which later became called 'Traitors' Gate'. Then on the right you can see him inside the White Tower. He is seated at a table, writing. You can also see him leaning rather sadly out of the window. Notice that since the time of William of Normandy the White Tower has been surrounded by two strong walls and many smaller towers. The Tower of London is in fact many towers. It was not a prison from which it would have been easy to escape.

Moving across to the castle yard, you can see the Duke greeting a messenger who has arrived with news that the ransom has been paid. Finally you can see the Duke riding out through the gates of the Tower. He is a free man!

Looking beyond the Tower the artist shows us a great deal about the London of his time. It is not a realistic view but he has drawn individual buildings carefully.

The green area on the right is *Tower Hill* which for many years became the place of execution.

The building with the archways underneath is probably *Billingsgate* which was famous for its fish market until it closed in 1982.

Stretching across the painting is London Bridge with its houses. On the extreme left you can see the Chapel to St Thomas à Becket which was built in the centre of the bridge.

At the top of the painting we can see a skyline of city churches. On the extreme left is the tower of St Paul's Cathedral.

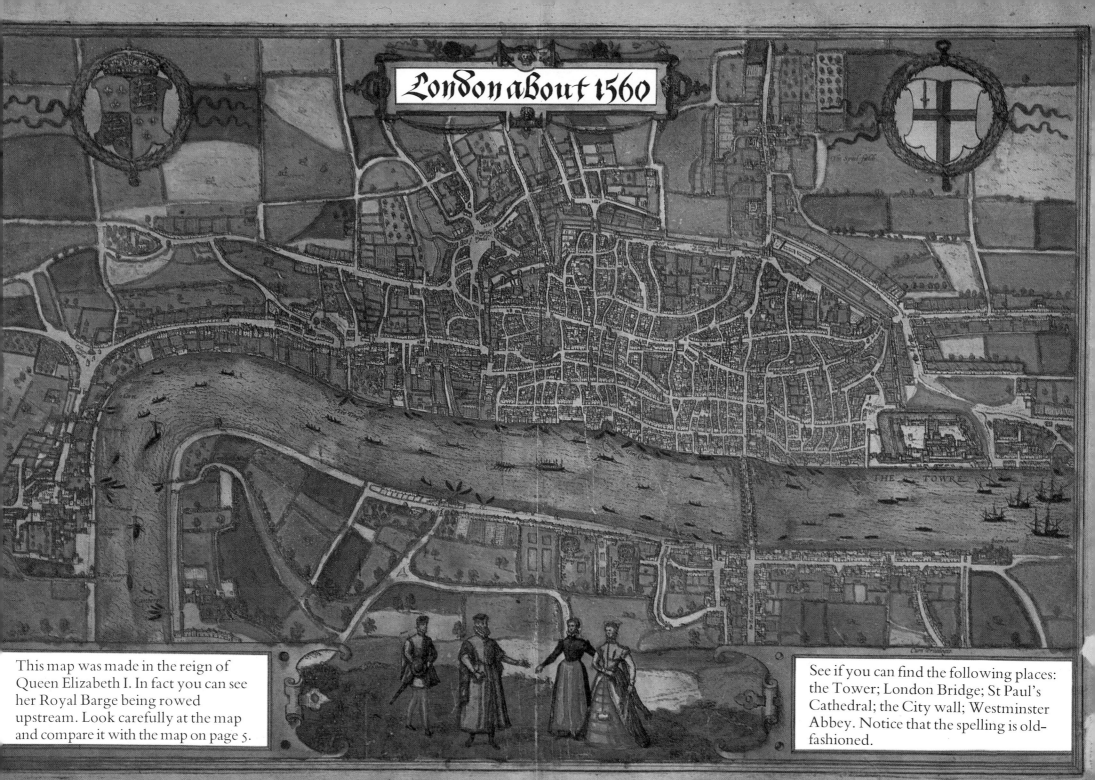

London about 1560

This map was made in the reign of Queen Elizabeth I. In fact you can see her Royal Barge being rowed upstream. Look carefully at the map and compare it with the map on page 5.

See if you can find the following places: the Tower; London Bridge; St Paul's Cathedral; the City wall; Westminster Abbey. Notice that the spelling is old-fashioned.

Tower of London

In 1598 a tailor called John Stow wrote this description of the Tower of London:

'*The City of London hath in the East a very great and mighty fortress whose towers rise from deep foundations. This tower is a citadel to defend or command the Citie: a royal palace for assemblies or treaties; a prison for the most dangerous offenders; the only place of coinage for all England at this time: the armoury for warlike provision; the treasury of the ornaments and jewels of the crown, and general conserver of the records of the King's Courts of Justice at Westminster.*'
Compare this view of the Tower with the recent photograph on page 4. What differences can you spot?

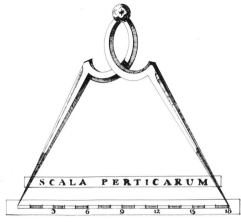

SCALA PERTICARUM

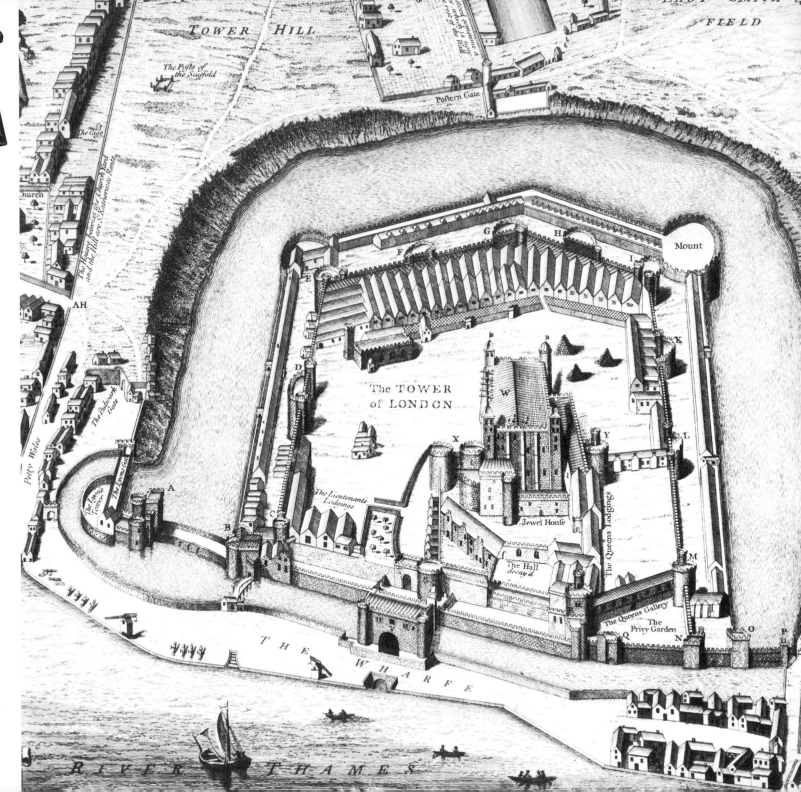

Moorfields 1559

If you walked across London Bridge and kept going roughly north, you would come to *Bishop's Gate*. In just 15 minutes' walk from the river, you would have crossed the city and be out in the fields beyond! It shows just how small London was at the start of the reign of the first Queen Elizabeth. (See the map on page 11.)

Beyond the gate the road continues north ①. It is lined by houses. The population of London is beginning to grow rapidly. It will double in the next 40 years to around 200,000 people. Some people have to live beyond the city walls. Some no doubt prefer it to the noise and bustle and smell of the city centre. Some of the houses have carefully laid out gardens and orchards ②. In the fields a good deal of work and play is going on. Laundry women are spreading out clothes to dry ③. Newly woven cloth is being stretched on special frames ④. Some men are practising their archery ⑤ while others are using firearms ⑥.

Can you spot the following: a woman carrying a pot on her head; two men riding the same horse; two wells; two windmills; two men carrying a basket of washing and a man leading a horse and cart driving what might be a couple of pigs?

In 1606 *Moorfields* was laid out as one of London's first parks. Today this area lies buried deep beneath Liverpool Street Station.

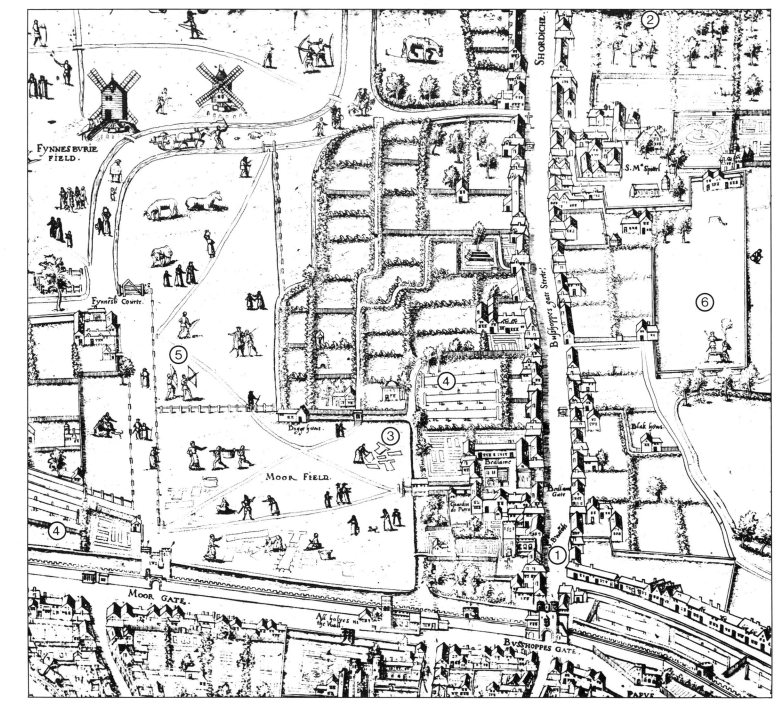

The Coronation Procession of Edward VI 1547

Every king and queen of England from Richard II in 1377 to Charles II in 1661 spent the night before their coronation in the chapel at the Tower of London praying for God's help. Then on the day of the coronation Londoners were able to enjoy a splendid procession as the new ruler travelled from the Tower in the east of London to Westminster Abbey for the crowning ceremony.

In this picture the artist has very cleverly managed to include the whole of the procession by exaggerating the size of the figures. On the left of the picture, the end of the procession is still leaving the Tower of London. Notice the curtain walls which surround the White Tower and the moat which is full of water. For many years in its history, the Tower was a royal palace as well as a fortress and a prison. The open space in front of the Tower is Tower Hill. Compare this scene with that on pages 2–3 which was drawn 300 years later.

Edward VI is a boy king. He is only nine years old. Unlike his father Henry VIII, Edward is weak and sickly and will not live long. You can see him in the centre of the picture. He is riding a white horse.

Above him a golden canopy is held by four outriders.

The road they are passing along is called *Cheapside*. The word cheap meant a market. In fact Cheapside was the home of the gold and silversmiths. You can see them displaying their goods as the procession goes by.

The big church on the right is old St Paul's Cathedral. Notice how much larger it is than the surrounding buildings.

Just to the right of St Paul's is *Ludgate*, one of the city's seven gateways.

The procession continues on to *Temple Bar* and past *Charing Cross*. Then on through open fields and gardens to Westminster.

If you look across the river to *Southwark* you can see that there are still very few people living there. The boatmen, however, are doing a good trade bringing people across the river to see the procession. Have another look at the map on page 11. Don't forget that the map is looking north, while this picture is looking south.

If we left the procession, crossed to the south bank and looked back at the City, what would we see?

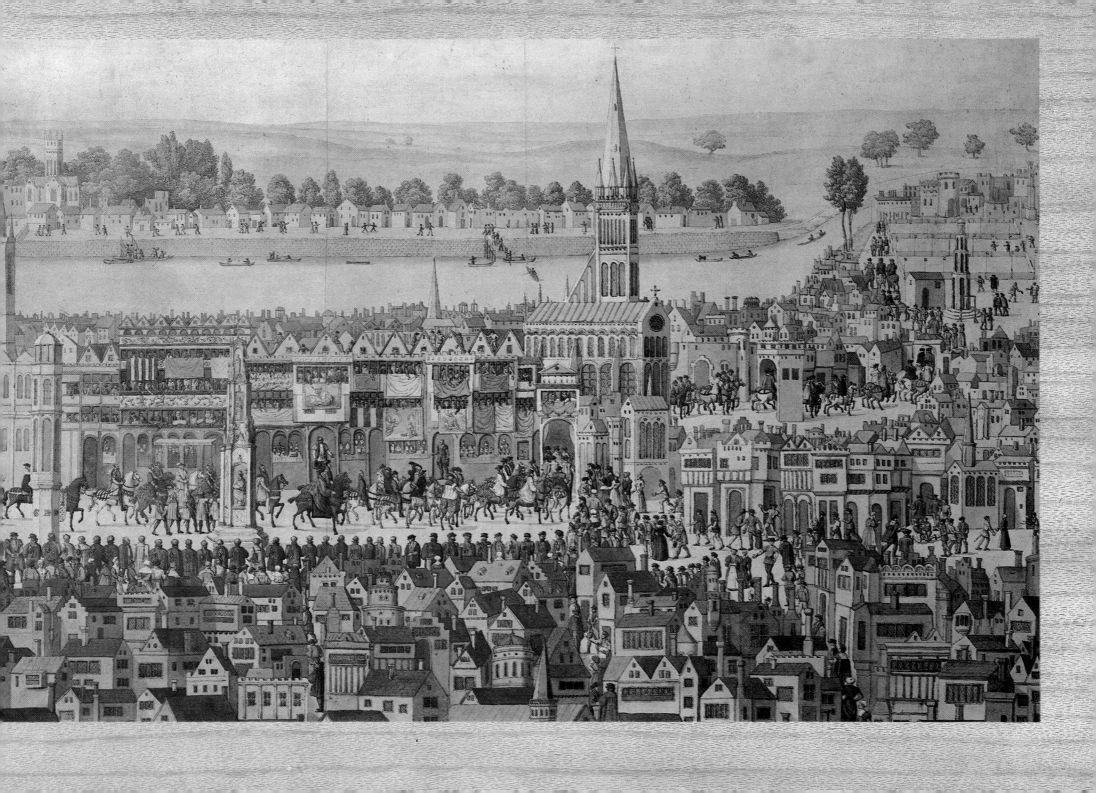

A PANORAMA *of the* CITY

This is a view of how London looked from Southwark south of the Thames. It was published in 1616 but was probably drawn some years earlier. The artist has exaggerated the height of the buildings but he still gives us a fascinating glimpse of London 400 years ago.

This is the London that William Shakespeare would have known. In fact in the bottom left hand corner you can see the theatre called the Globe ① where many of his plays were performed. Nearby is another place of entertainment the Bear Garden ②. Here powerful dogs called mastiffs would be used to fight bulls and bears. Both the Globe and the Bear Garden are flying flags which indicated that the show was about to begin.

Across the river the scene is dominated by St Pauls ③. Notice the spire has gone. It was struck by lightning in 1561 and nobody bothered to repair it. On the far left you can see a windmill ④. At this time the wind was still an important source of power. Moving east along the wharfs and steps we can see a number of cranes being used to unload goods and perhaps weigh them. At *Queenhithe* there is a water tower ⑤ which provided a limited water supply for houses in the west of the city.

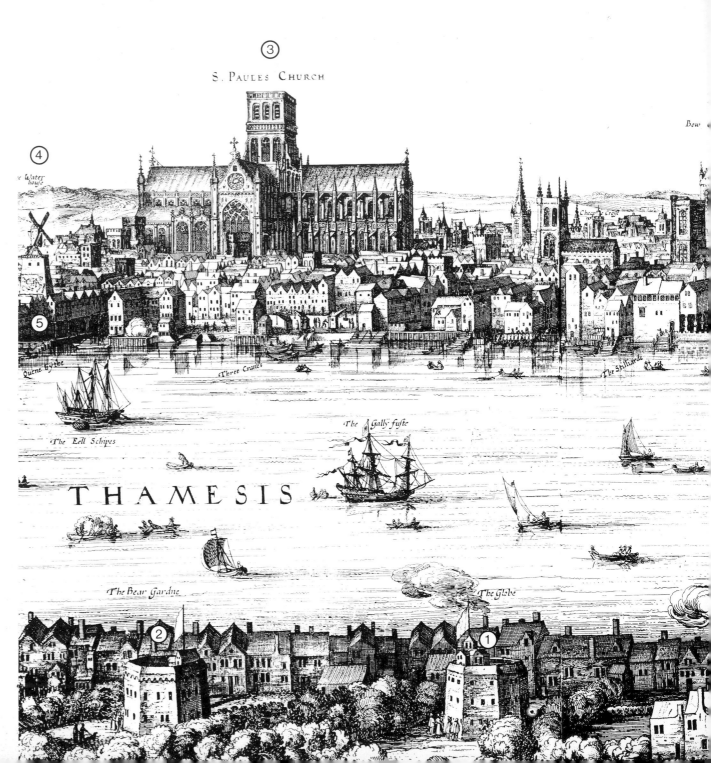

S. PAULES CHURCH

THAMESIS

In the foreground on the left you can see a busy scene ①. If you look closely you can see market stalls and some dangerous-looking, long-horned cattle. A man is running after a cart and another man is pushing a barrel on a barrow. The coach is a forerunner of the stage-coach. It has no springs and must be very uncomfortable. There is a woman with a child, and a man relieving himself against a wall! No one seems concerned about the rotting heads mounted on spikes above the gate house ②. They were put there as a dreadful warning to the enemies of the government that the punishment for treason was death.

At the time this drawing was made London Bridge was already 400 years old. It was started in 1176 and completed in 1209. The picture isn't totally accurate. The arches were pointed and varied in size ③. Two of the arches on the northern side were fitted with water wheels ④ which operated pumps that supplied the city with water.

In the river a boat has lowered its mast as it has just passed under the bridge ⑤. This could be a dangerous operation when the tide was going out. The bridge constricted the flow of water and produced strong currents. Every year people drowned trying to 'shoot the bridge' as it was called.

Downstream of the bridge there are many more ships including some large ones of the type that fought against the Spanish Armada. On the north bank you can see a mass of shipping off-loading their cargoes at the *Legal Quays* ⑥ where custom duties had to be paid to officials of the Custom-house before goods could be imported into the country.

Near the centre of the picture you can see the Tower of London ⑦. Tower Wharf stands out clearly with a number of cannons in position ⑧.

The area south of the river ⑨ now lies under London Bridge Station. HMS *Belfast* is now moored approximately here ⑩. (See pages 62–3.)

19

L·O·N·D·O·N B·R·I·D·G·E

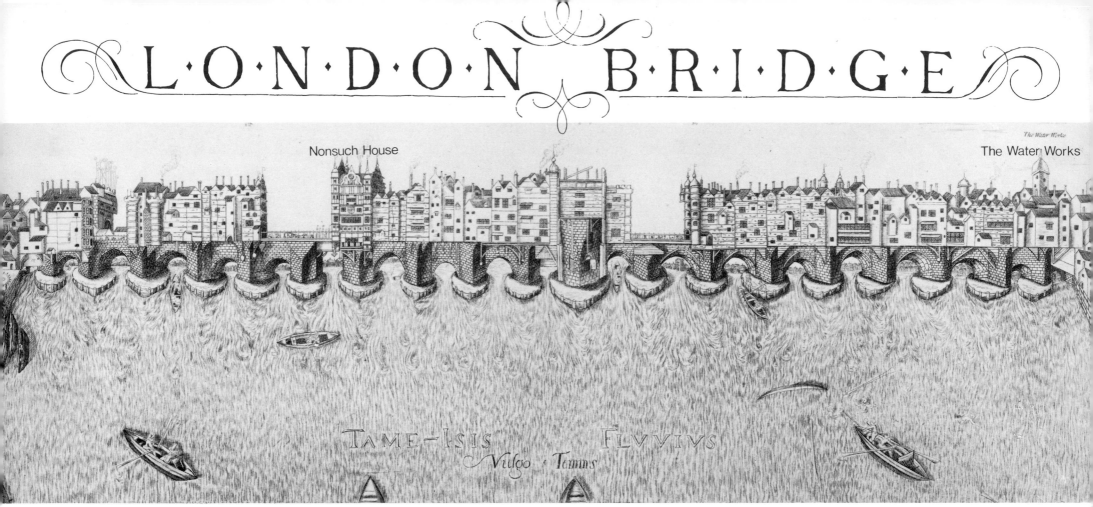

Nonsuch House

The Water Works

TAME-ISIS FLVVIVS
Vulgo · Temnis

SOUTH BANK

NORTH BANK

London Bridge was regarded by people at the time as one of the great wonders of the world. '*Comparable itself to a little city*,' said John Norden who engraved this picture at the end of the reign of Queen Elizabeth I. The original intention had been that the rents of the houses and shops would pay for keeping the bridge in good repair. The bridge was 350 yards long (320m). The width of the road was only 12ft (3.66m) which made it very crowded and congested. Not only was the roadway lined with shops, there were also street traders offering their wares. Occasionally a herd of cattle would be driven across and everyone would have to dive for a doorway or be trampled under foot. The bridge contributed greatly to London's wealth because it channelled so much trade into the city.

In this illustration we are looking west. Can you see the Chapel to St Thomas à Becket, Nonsuch House and the drawbridge?

Because the Bridge restricted the flow of water, the river Thames sometimes froze over. In particularly bad winters the ice was sufficiently thick to enable a fair to be held on the river itself. The sketch on the opposite page gives you an idea of some of the things people got up to. Examine it carefully. We are looking north towards *the Temple*. A street of stalls and booths has been erected across the ice. There is even a printing press at work. On the left an ox is being roasted. Various coaches are rushing to and fro. Some of the boatmen who normally row people across the river have put wheels or skids on their boats to keep themselves in business. Can you see people playing nine-pins, watching a bull being baited, hunting a fox and playing football? This picture was drawn during the great freeze of 1683–84.

FROST FAIRS ON THE THAMES

◀ A Wedding Feast at Bermondsey 1571

Across the river from the Tower of London lies *Bermondsey*. Here preparations are being made for a feast to celebrate a wedding.

On the extreme right a party of people dressed very formally in black are approaching from the church. Four fiddlers are providing some lively music and a group of young people appear to have started dancing. Behind them in a barn a long table has been laid. In the next building a lot of cooking is going on. Four enormous cakes or pies are being displayed.

The artist who painted this picture was a Dutchman called Joris Hoefnagel. He makes his buildings look rather foreign. However, he drew the details of people's clothes very carefully. On the left-hand side of the painting he shows the guests arriving. They are altogether more brightly dressed than the people on the right.

Preaching at Paul's Cross 1616 ▶

Paul's Cross stood at the north-west corner of old St Paul's Cathedral. Beneath the cross is a pulpit from which bishops could preach to a huge open-air congregation. Frequently the sermon was used by the government to make important announcements. Of course, this was long before the days of radio or television or daily newspapers. Sometimes items of important news were read out here—news perhaps of a victory or a new law or even an appeal for money. St Paul's was in a very poor state of repair at this time and in 1620 King James I launched an appeal for money to restore the cathedral. In fact this picture may have been drawn to advertise the appeal. The artist, however, shows us the cathedral in a far better state than it actually was.

You can see King James and Queen Anne in their box in the centre of the picture. Beneath them listening to the sermon is the Lord Mayor and some of the Aldermen of the City of London. In the City of London the Lord Mayor is always regarded as the most important person apart from the King or Queen! In the picture see if you can see the 'dog catcher' whose job it was to stop stray dogs interfering with people and disturbing the service. Another small detail to notice is a set of steps used to help people mount their horses. Notice all the birds flying about. The huge old cathedral must have been home for a great many of them. Finally can you spot the 'hour glass'? What do you think that was used for?

The Plague

Ring-a-ring 'o roses
A pocket full of posies
A-tishoo!, A-tishoo!
We all fall down.

By 1665 the population of London had reached 400,000. It was by far the largest city in England. In fact one person in 12 lived here. Many country people thought London was a dirty, overcrowded and unhealthy place which was best avoided.

The problem was that 400,000 people living close together produce a great deal of rubbish and waste. As yet no one had devised a satisfactory means of getting rid of it. Today there are a great many rules and regulations controlling how towns are run. There are also many officials to make sure these rules are obeyed. In the 17th century this was not the case. If a butcher had a lot of stinking offal to get rid of, like as not he would just dump it in the nearest convenient spot. Surprising as it may seem to us, people then did not connect dirt with disease. After all, London streets had never been noted for their cleanliness

and that had never prevented London being the most prosperous town in the country.

The plague was a dreadful disease. It was spread by a type of flea which lived on black rats. In the narrow streets and the uncovered sewers there was plenty of rubbish on which the rats could thrive. And thrive they did.

The last great outbreak of the plague started in the winter of 1664–5 in an area called *St Giles* which lay to the west of the City and north of Charing Cross. By the following summer it had spread to the rest of London. At its height people were dying at the rate of 5,000 a week. The disease affected people like this: the victim would become feverish; bumps would appear in the groin and armpits and a rose-coloured rash would appear on the body. Sometimes people collapsed very suddenly.

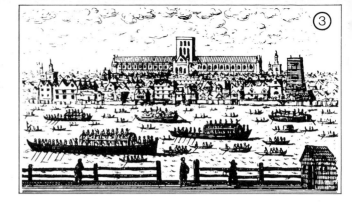

The rough drawings on this page tell the story of the terrible year of the Great Plague. Few people ever recovered from the Plague.

Few doctors had any idea of what to do. Whole families were shut up together: the dead, the sick and the well. In these conditions the disease spread quickly and whole families died.

The City Council insisted that red crosses were to be painted on the doors of houses where people were ill. They ordered that all the cats and dogs be killed but this did more harm than good as these were the very animals that hunted the rats. 'Searchers' were appointed to seek out victims and make sure they did not leave their homes. People lit bonfires in the streets to keep the plague away. Others carried bunches of strong herbs.

A generall Bill for this prefent year, ending the 19 of *December* 1665. according to the Report made to the KINGS moft Excellent Majefty.

By the Company of Parifh Clerks of *London*, &c.

The Difeafes and Cafualties this year.

Abortive and Stilborne	617	Executed	21
Aged	1545	Flox and Small Pox	655
Ague and Feaver	5257	Found dead in ftreets, fields, &c.	20
Appoplex and Suddenly	116	French Pox	86
Bedrid	10	Frighted	23
Blafted	5	Gout and Sciatica	27
Bleeding	16	Grief	46
Bloody Flux, Scowring & Flux	185	Griping in the Guts	1288
Burnt and Scalded	8	Hang'd & made away themfelves	7
Calenture	3	Headmould fhot & Mould fallen	14
Cancer, Gangrene and Fiftula	56	Jaundies	110
Canker, and Thrufh	111	Impoftume	227
Childbed	625	Kil'd by feverall accidents	46
Chrifomes and Infants	1258	Kings Evill	86
Cold and Cough	68	Leprofie	2
Collick and Winde	134	Lethargy	14
Confumption and Tiffick	4808	Livergrown	20
Convulfion and Mother	2036	Meagrom and Headach	12
Diftracted	5	Meafles	7
Dropfie and Timpany	1478	Murthered and Shot	9
Drowned	50	Overlaid & Starved	45

Palfie	30		
Plague	68596		
Plannet	6		
Plurifie	15		
Poyfoned	1		
Quinfie	35		
Rickets	557		
Rifing of the Lights	397		
Rupture	34		
Scurvy	105		
Shingles and Swine pox	2		
Sores, Ulcers, broken and bruifed Limbs	82		
Spleen	14		
Spotted Feaver and Purples	1929		
Stopping of the ftomack	332		
Stone and Strangury	98		
Surfet	1251		
Teeth and Worms	2614		
Vomiting	51		
VVenn	8		

Chriftned { Males — 5114, Females — 4853, In all — 9967 }
Buried { Males — 48569, Females — 48737, In all — 97306 } Of the Plague — 68596

Increased in the Burials in the 130 Parifhes and at the Peft-houfe this year — 79009
Increased of the Plague in the 130 Parifhes and at the Peft-houfe this year — 68590

Many of those who could afford to left London. This made life even worse for those who were left behind, because trade came to a standstill and it was difficult for people who were still well to earn any money.

Each night carts came round to pick up the bodies of those who had died. Before long the carts came by day as well. There were soon problems about where to bury the dead. New graveyards were constructed in *Finsbury Fields* and *Highgate*.

As autumn approached the numbers dying began to drop. By December it was all over. Those who had fled returned. The plague itself never did. The official death-toll was given as 68,596 people. The true figure may have been much higher because not all the deaths were recorded.

Carts full of dead to bury.

Scenes from the Plague

The Great Fire of London

Early in the morning of Sunday 2 September 1666 fire breaks out in the house of Thomas Farrinor in *Pudding Lane*. A strong wind is blowing from the east and the flames leap easily from house to house. Many of the buildings are wooden and covered in pitch. They burn well.

The fire continues until Wednesday when the wind drops and effective fire-breaks are finally constructed. By this time St Paul's has been destroyed along with 84 churches and 13,000 homes.

In the foreground of the painting, the artist illustrates people struggling to save some of their property. In the centre of the painting stands St Paul's. Although it seems surrounded by flames the fire has not yet taken hold. Its roof is untouched. Silhouetted on the right is the Tower of London. The Tower was used as a gun powder store. Had the flames reached it there would have been a terrible explosion. Samuel Pepys watched the progress of the fire from the Tower. Here is an extract from the description he wrote in his diary: '*The houses on this end of the Bridge are all on fire. People are endeavouring to remove their goods and property, throwing them in the river or bringing them off in small boats. Poor people stay in their houses until the fire reaches them. Then they go running and clambering from one pair of stairs by the water side to another. And the poor pigeons are also loathe to leave their houses but hover about the windows and balconies until they burn their wings and fall down. As I watch a high and mighty wind drives the fire towards the city and nobody to my sight endeavours to quench it.*'

27

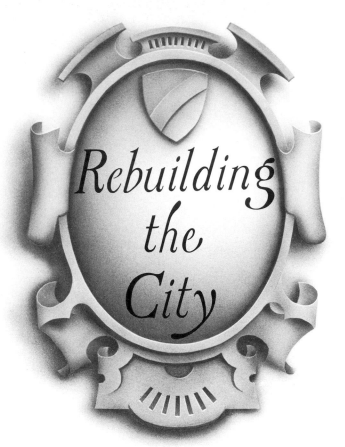

Rebuilding the City

The Monument was built in 1677 near Pudding Lane as a permanent reminder of the fire. It is 202 feet high (61m). On the top above the viewing platform stands a vase of flames.

The Fire of London was a great disaster but it provided an extraordinary opportunity to rebuild a much cleaner, healthier, less overcrowded city. However, everybody had different ideas about how this could be achieved.

The main problem was that the City had to be got back to work again as quickly as possible before people took their skills and looked for jobs elsewhere.

In the end all the grand plans for a new city were abandoned. By and large the old medieval street pattern was kept. In some cases roads were widened so there was room for both pedestrians and vehicles. Raised pavements were introduced for the first time. The government insisted that only stone or brick-built buildings could be put up and they controlled how high these could be. People were prevented from building upper stories jutting out over the road as had happened in the past. The façades or fronts of buildings had to be flat. Water spouts which splashed water over passers-by were banned. Gutters and down-pipes had to be used to carry away rain water.

Not everybody returned to live in the City. Poorer people could not afford the higher rents charged for the fine, new brick buildings. Some traders and craftsmen preferred to live outside the city where they could avoid the rules and regulations of the City Council. But of course, many people did return and very rapidly the business life of the City got back to normal.

Compare the view of London on the opposite page with those on pages 16–17 and 62–3. The white area on the map shows how much of London was destroyed by the Great Fire.

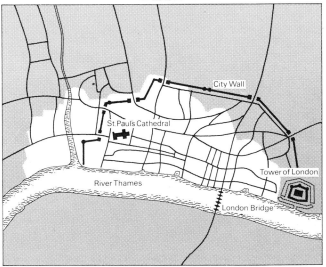

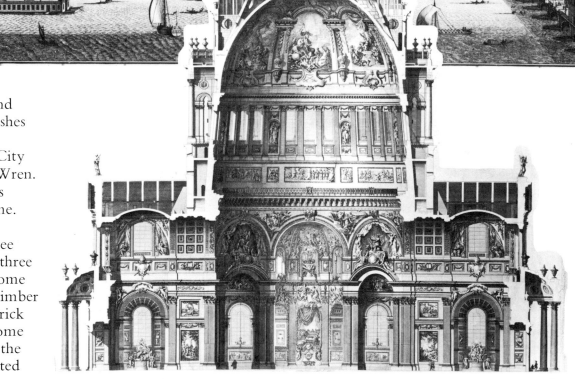

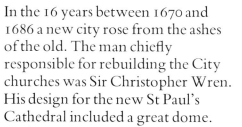

In the 16 years between 1670 and 1686 a new city rose from the ashes of the old. The man chiefly responsible for rebuilding the City churches was Sir Christopher Wren. His design for the new St Paul's Cathedral included a great dome.

If you look at the cut-away diagram on the right you will see that the famous dome is in fact three domes. First there is an outer dome made of metal supported by a timber framework. Beneath that is a brick cone and inside that an inner dome which provided the ceiling for the church below. On this are painted some splendid pictures. Above the dome is a stone lantern and cross.

Huge amounts of material were needed to rebuild the cathedral. More than 30,000 tons of stone were brought by barge from Portland. Also needed were 23,000 tons of other stone, wagon loads of timber, marble, chalk, iron and lead. The money for all this was raised by a nationwide appeal and a tax on coal.

In October 1709 the last stone was set in place by Wren's son, 34 years after the Foundation stone had been laid. The new St Paul's dramatically changed the London skyline.

The Horseferry c.1706 ▶

Can you work out where this picture was painted? In the distance beyond the bend in the river you can see the new St Paul's Cathedral surrounded by the spires of Sir Christopher Wren's many churches. The building across the river from us is *Lambeth Palace*, the London home of the Archbishop of Canterbury. In fact we are in the City of Westminster where Lambeth Bridge is today.

At the start of the 18th century Westminster was growing rapidly but still there was only the one bridge two miles downstream. The only way to cross the river at Westminster was to use the horseferry, unless of course you were prepared to swim. There were fixed charges: a man and horse two pence; a horse and chaise one shilling; a coach and two horses one shilling and sixpence; a laden cart two shillings.

The citizens of London were not keen on the idea of a new bridge because they thought they would lose trade. The watermen who operated the ferries and who provided a water taxi service were sure it would ruin them. Notice the girl dancing, she is wearing a traditional May Day head-dress.

Westminster by Canaletto c.1750 ▶

Now we have crossed the river to Lambeth and are looking back towards Westminster. You can still see the slipway used by the horseferry in the foreground but the ferry has gone out of business. It was no longer needed after Westminster Bridge was built. Just to the left of the bridge you can see a row of trees. Behind them are the *Houses of Parliament*. Beyond you can see the roof of Westminster Hall. The bridge was a great success. No houses were built on top of it and traffic flowed freely. Before long the City of London followed Westminster's example and knocked down all the houses on their bridge

Old Custom House Quay 1751

By the middle of the 18th century London was growing enormously wealthy. One of the main reasons for this was trade. Once upon a time goods brought into Britain from abroad could only be afforded by the rich. Now quite ordinary people wanted things from foreign lands: things like tea and coffee; sugar; cotton and silk.

The government put a tax on everything imported into the country. This tax or custom duty had to be paid before a cargo could be sold.

In this painting by Samuel Scott, a ship's captain is being interviewed by a customs-official. The official is probably checking that the captain is not trying to smuggle goods into the country without paying the correct duty. Nearby two workmen are opening up some barrels to see what they contain. The captain looks rather bored. Goods could only be unloaded on the 'legal quays' which lay between the Tower and the Bridge. As a result the river got very crowded and sometimes it took weeks before a ship could unload. Sometimes the cargo went bad, or was spoiled or stolen.

By the end of the 18th century a solution had to be found to this problem because delays and over-crowding were beginning to discourage the very trade which had made London so rich.

Have another look at the painting. The large wheel in the background is a tread-wheel. The wheel is turned by a gang of men walking along inside it. As the wheel turns it winds up a rope. In this way heavy cargoes could be winched up into the storerooms.

Notice the ships with their vast sails. Many men were needed to sail them. The journeys they made to the East were long and dangerous. However, the profits that could be made were equally great. But sadly not everybody shared London's growing wealth.

GIN·LANE

William Hogarth's London

Gin Lane is an imaginary street, but the problems of the people who live there were very real.

In the first half of the 18th century gin became very cheap. The saying went: drunk for a penny; dead drunk for twopence; clean straw for nothing. Nobody needed a licence to sell gin. Anybody could open up a gin shop. Not surprisingly many people drank far too much, particularly the poorer people. Look at Hogarth's picture. In the foreground a man has almost starved himself to death. His body is virtually a skeleton. His shoes no longer fit. A drunken woman is unaware that her baby has slipped from her grasp. On the left two hungry beggars have stolen a bone from a dog. A little above them a young couple deal with a pawn broker. He hands over the tools of his trade and she parts with her cooking pots. Hogarth suggests that the money the pawn broker gives them will be spent on drink. Notice how well kept the pawn broker's house is. What other buildings are also well-preserved? All the other buildings are in poor shape or are actually collapsing. In one ruined building a man has committed suicide.

Even the young are not safe from the perils of gin drinking. On the right-hand side of the engraving a mother gives her baby gin to soothe it. Nearby two small girls pour gin for each other.

Poverty and drunkenness led to crime. In 18th century London there were a great many crimes for which you could be sentenced to hang. Stealing a handkerchief could be a hanging offence. Children were sometimes punished in the same way as adults. The place of execution was *Tyburn* where Marble Arch now stands. Prisoners would be brought by cart from *Newgate Prison*. People would leave their work to watch the procession go by.

At almost exactly the same time as the Italian artist Antonio Canaletto was painting his bright sunlit views of London, a London artist called William Hogarth was drawing very different pictures. He recorded the grim lives that people led in the crowded back-streets of London which lay between the City and Westminster.

An Execution at Tyburn

Executions were public affairs. Many people came to watch. A grandstand was sometimes put up to make sure everyone got a good view. Broadsheets detailing the careers of the prisoners and their farewell speech always sold well.

The victim would be made to stand on the back of a flat cart. A rope would be placed round his or her neck. The cart would be driven off leaving the victim to hang. The body would belong to the hangman to dispose of as he wished.

Can you see the hangman? He is on top of the gallows quietly smoking his pipe. On the right you can see a famous street trader of 18th century London. His name was Tiddy Doll. He sold gingerbread. What else is going on?

BARTHOLOMEW FAIR, 1721.

This Fair was granted by Henry the 1st, to one Rahere, a witty and pleasant gentleman of his Court, in aid and for the support of an Hospital, Priory and Church, dedicated to St. Bartholomew, which he built in repentance of his former profligacy and folly. The succeeding Priors claimed, by certain Charters, to have a Fair every year, during three days, viz: on the Eve, the Day, and on the Marrow of St. Bartholomew. At this period the Clothiers of England, and Drapers of London, kept their Booths and Standings there, and a Court of Piepowder was held daily for the Settlement of all Debts and Contracts. About the year 1721, when the present interesting View of this popular Fair was taken, the Drama was considered of some importance, and a series of minor although regular Pieces were acted in its various Booths. At Lee and Harper's the Siege of Bethulia is performing, in which is introduced the Tragedy of Holifernia. Persons of Rank were also its occasional visiters, and the figure on the right is supposed to be that of Sir Robert Walpole, then Prime Minister. Fawkes, the famous conjuror, forms a conspicuous feature, and is the only portrait of him known to exist. The remaining amusements are not unlike those of our day, except in the articles of Hollands and Gin, with which the lower orders were then accustomed to indulge unfettered by license or excise.

Published as the Act directs by J. F. Setchel, 23, King-Street, Covent-Garden.

BARTHOLOMEW FAIR

◀ Southwark Fair 1733

London's fairs and markets provided a great deal of entertainment for free or for only a few pence. Southwark Fair was always held in September. Large numbers of performers would arrive to entertain the crowd. In the painting on the left by William Hogarth you can see some of the shows on offer at Southwark Fair.

Starting at the bottom left-hand corner of the picture, a frightening looking man rides through the crowd to challenge volunteers to a fight. Just to the right is a peep-show. It costs a farthing to take a look. In the centre a group of strolling players make a grand entry. The woman beats the drum to gather an audience while a boy plays a trumpet. Unfortunately the actor dressed in armour looks as if he is being arrested. In front of the china stall a man is gambling away his money. In the bottom right-hand corner is a boy playing the bagpipes.

Nearby, the stage above the china stall has collapsed and a tangle of actors and musicians are falling through the roof.

Meanwhile across the road another play is in progress. A large sign showing a wooden horse announces that the play is about the Siege of Troy.

These old London fairs caused a great deal of disturbance and attracted many criminals. Southwark Fair was banned in 1762 and Bartholomew Fair in 1855.

Vauxhall Pleasure Gardens

The West End

More than 250 years ago, Daniel Defoe, the author of *Robinson Crusoe*, asked '*And whither will this monstrous city extend?*'. He was right to be concerned. London was growing very rapidly. To the west of the city, where once there had been fields, elegant squares were being constructed. And of course families like the Grosvenors who owned these fields made great fortunes.

The squares were all laid out in a similar fashion with a small park in the centre and buildings on all four sides. The houses usually had five floors and were very grand with ballrooms and spacious reception rooms on the lower floors. Below street level were basements for the kitchens. Under the roof were the attics for the servants. Huge numbers of servants were needed to run these large houses and of course this attracted yet more people to come to London to find work and perhaps make a fortune. By 1801 the population of London had risen to 900,000.

◄ **Vauxhall Pleasure Gardens 1784**

On summer evenings fashionable Londoners would cross the Thames by boat to visit the Vauxhall Pleasure Gardens. Here they could walk down avenues of trees beneath coloured lanterns. They could have dinner with their friends and listen to the music of George Frederick Handel, one of the most popular composers of the time. Seated at the table you can see two famous inhabitants of London, Dr Johnson and his friend James Boswell.

What do you think the artist thought about the people he was drawing?

While the fashionable West End was growing, important developments were taking place in the commercial East End of London.

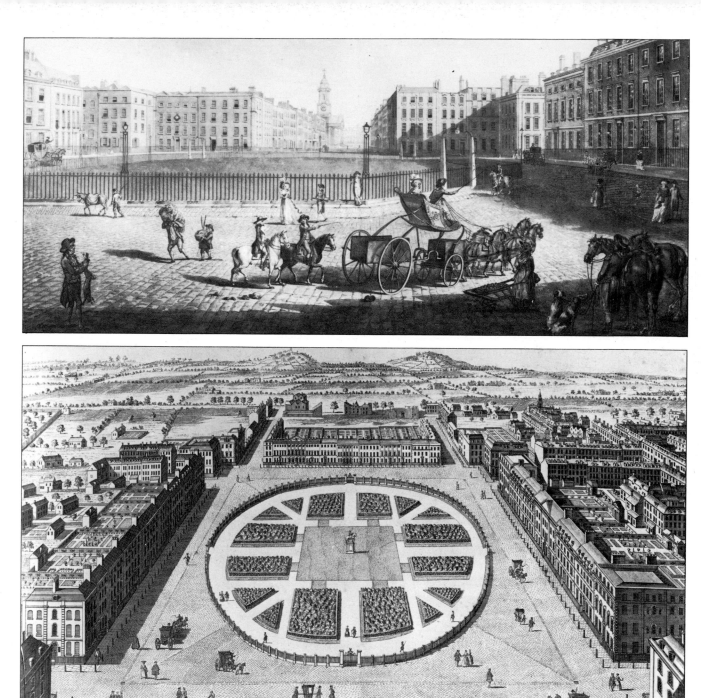

TOP Hanover Square 1787   ABOVE Grosvenor Square 1731

The Pool of London 1804

While money was spent in the fashionable West End, it was in the East End that money was made. More money could have been made if the river Thames had not been so crowded. If you look at the picture above you will see a mass of shipping waiting to unload at the Legal Quays (see page 31). In fact many ships had to off-load their cargoes for lighters or barges to bring ashore.

The answer to all this congestion was to build specially designed wet docks. At the top of page 39 you can see an engraving of Howland Great Dock which was the largest dock on the river throughout the 18th century. It had room for berthing, building or repairing 120 merchant ships. If you look carefully you will see a ship being *warped* through the dock gate. However it was still forbidden to unload cargoes here.

Finally, in 1799, Parliament decided it must get rid of the out-of-date laws governing the docks which were now in danger of damaging London's trade. In the next thirty years the government gave permission for the construction of a whole series of docks, downstream of the Tower of London, which would reduce congestion and enable cargoes to be unloaded more quickly.

LONDON DOCKS

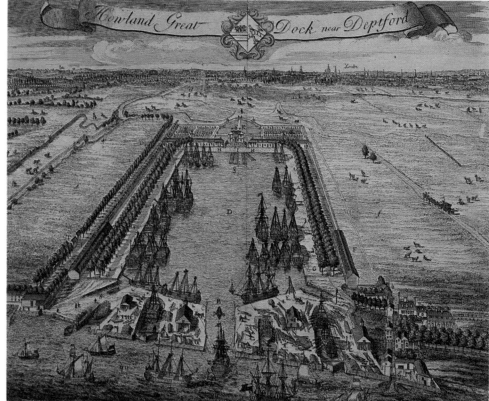

The docks were deep so that the ships could come alongside the quay to off-load their cargo. Huge gates kept the water in the docks so that the ships were not affected by the rising and falling of the tide. Large warehouses were constructed next to the quay so that goods could be stored safely. Around the docks a high wall would be built to keep out robbers.

In the picture below, the artist shows us the West India Docks looking west towards the city. You can just make out St Paul's Cathedral in the distance. On the right is the Import Dock busy with ships bringing goods into the country. In the centre is the Export Dock where ships are loading goods to take out of the country. Can you see the dock gates? Why are they in pairs? On the left of the illustration is the City Canal. This was designed as a short cut to avoid ships having to sail all round the Isle of Dogs. The ships were hauled through the Canal by gangs of men. Unfortunately the Canal was not a commercial success. Eventually it was also turned into a dock. (You can see the docks from the air on page 53.)

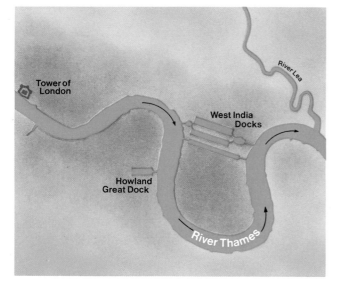

LONDON going out of Town. — or — The March of Bricks & Mortar!

London going out of Town ◄

The artist who drew this cartoon was George Cruikshank. George lived in *Islington* on the northern edge of London. The back of his house had always overlooked open countryside. Then in 1829 the builders arrived. To get as much profit as possible the builder would cram his buildings as close together as he could. Look at the cartoon. What might make you think that these new houses are not well built?

Between 1800 and 1850 the population of London increased from just under one million to two and a half million. Perhaps the main reason why London grew so rapidly was the coming of the railways.

Over London by Rail 1872 ►

Wherever a railway station opened, houses quickly followed. Very rapidly the small villages surrounding London were swallowed up by mile upon mile of new housing.

While the railways brought great benefits, thousands of people lived in their shadow. London had always been a dirty, smoky place. Generations of Londoners complained about it. Now London became far more sooty. Buildings turned black and grimy. Trying to dry washing must have been a hopeless task. Notice that the railway line is built on brick arches to save the expense of demolishing existing buildings.

41

The Victorians thought the railways were very exciting. They thought that riding on a train was as exciting as we find flying in an aeroplane. William Frith spent a whole year working on this painting. It includes a great deal of detail for you to explore.

Start with the station itself. Notice that vast great roof and all the attractive iron work. Even the lamps are well designed. The railway companies made their London stations as impressive as they could to encourage people to travel by train.

Now look at the train. Notice that the carriages still look like horse-drawn coaches. Even the luggage is being loaded on top. The train is divided into first, second and third class carriages which are next to the engine where they are likely to be very smoky. As far as we can see these carriages were little better than goods vans.

Now look at the passengers. On the extreme right a man is being arrested by two detectives. What has he done? We can only imagine. One detective carries a warrant. The other carries a pair of hand-cuffs.

To their left, a newly married couple are setting off on their honeymoon. A servant touches his top hat to the bridegroom. The women wear shawls, poke bonnets and crinolines which are supported by wire hoops. The children are dressed as elaborately as the adults. These are well-to-do people. In the foreground a porter dressed in green stoops to pick up some luggage. Behind him a soldier in a scarlet uniform kisses his baby goodbye. Has the soldier been posted abroad to some distant part of Queen Victoria's Empire? Again we don't know. The artist invites us to imagine a story.

In the centre of the painting a foreign-looking gentleman appears to be having an argument with the cabby who has brought him to the station. Perhaps he thinks he has been overcharged. He is carrying binoculars. Where do you think he and his wife are going?

Moving again to the foreground you can see a mother kissing her son. The two boys are being sent off to boarding school. The older one is holding a cricket bat and looking rather superior. Perhaps he thinks he is too old to be kissed.

On the left a porter pushes a loaded barrow through the crowd. Behind him come some second class passengers. They may have got held up in the traffic and are late. The boy is carrying a favourite toy. What is it?

Look at the painting carefully. How many porters can you see? How many paper boys? What sort of hats are the men wearing? Can you spot a sailor? How do the girls' dresses differ from those of the women?

PADDINGTON STATION 1862

OMNIBUS LIFE IN LONDON

◀ In the picture on the left we get a glimpse into a London omnibus. Everybody is very squashed together. It's made worse by their clothes which tend to be bulky and take up a lot of room. The conductor is trying to get the passengers to move up to make room for just one more. Notice that even he is wearing a top hat. Bus conductors were famous for the way they packed people in. They were often referred to as 'cads'. Unlike the railways there were no separate classes. The buses could be used by anybody who could pay the fare. 'Omnibus' is the Latin word meaning 'for everybody'. Today we have shortened it to plain and simple 'bus'.

George Shillibeer's Omnibus 1829 ▶

The first London bus service was introduced in 1829 by a man called George Shillibeer. He charged people 1s 6d ($7\frac{1}{2}$p) to take them from *Paddington* to the *Bank of England*. His vehicle was pulled by three horses and could carry approximately 20 people. Although stage coaches had previously existed, these operated from town to town. The horse buses were intended to carry people over much shorter distances. Notice that unlike a stage coach people got in at the back. The driver sat high up at the front giving him a clear view of the road ahead. By the 1830s there were many rival bus companies competing with each other. This added to London's traffic jams.

A Victorian Traffic Jam 1870 ▶

Sometimes we think that traffic jams are a fact of modern life. This is not true. In Victorian London the jams were as bad as the ones with which we are familiar today. Most roads were narrow. Sheep and cows would be driven through the streets to the main meat market at *Smithfield*.

This illustration shows the view down Fleet Street and up Ludgate Hill towards St Paul's. There used to be a bridge over the river Fleet at this spot. However the river became very polluted and it was arched over in the 18th century. Today it is still used as a sewer.

Look at all the different sorts of transport. In the foreground is a knifeboard omnibus. It was called this after the narrow board on which knives were cleaned. Passengers on the top deck had to sit back to back. London bus drivers were always complaining that they were overworked. *'The horses get one day's rest in four; but it's no rest for the driver. I never have time to look out for a wife.'*

If you thought the bus would be too slow you could take a London hansom cab. This was a two-wheeled vehicle in which the passenger sat under a hood and the driver sat above and behind the hood. How many such cabs can you see in the illustration?

Notice the gas lamp. Street lighting was first introduced in the early years of the 19th century. These lamps provided only a dim light in the smoky air.

The noise of all this traffic must have been incredible, because not only were the horses shod with iron but so were the wagon wheels.

Because of all the horse droppings many people earned money as crossing sweepers, although how people ever crossed this road is not easy to understand.

When lots of people live close together as they do in a large city, the problem of feeding them is enormous. Very little food can be produced in the city itself because there isn't enough room. So the food has to be bought from outside in huge quantities. Very early on in the history of London markets were set up where shopkeepers and traders could come to buy their supplies.

Billingsgate became famous in the 19th century for being London's main fish market. The market was also famous for the bad language of the people who worked there. On the left you can see an auctioneer busy auctioning baskets of small fish which an assistant is holding up for all to see.

Several people are trying to catch the auctioneer's eye to make their bids.

Notice the curious shaped hats of the porters. These were designed to help them lift heavy weights. They were called bobbing hats because that is how much the porters charged to carry the fish, a bob or one shilling (5p).

46

Billingsgate Market 1861

The artist who painted the picture on the left gives us a good impression of what the market was like. But he has left out all the anger, the bad language and the smell. Everybody looks very polite, and well-behaved. It's hard to imagine any of these people swearing. Notice that there is no rubbish. Everything is carefully arranged.

Although Victorian London was full of a great deal of poverty, dirt and disease, Victorian artists rarely recorded it. Notice the boy in the centre offering to carry the woman's basket. Perhaps he is an orphan. Perhaps he is homeless. Perhaps he is hungry. Victorian London was full of such children. Like all the paintings we have seen, this one only tells us part of the truth.

St Martin in the Fields 1888 ▶

This painting is a little more realistic. It contrasts the lives of two little girls. One walks with her well-dressed mother. The other is poorly dressed and already earning her living selling flowers. One girl has a life of luxury. The other has to get up early to go to the flower market to buy her basket of flowers. Perhaps she may not be allowed to go home until all her flowers are sold and she has made a profit. Many children in Victorian London led lives like this.

In the background of the picture you can see lots of interesting details. On the extreme right a street-sweeper stops at a coffee stall. Nearby a brewer's dray rumbles by loaded with beer barrels. On the left a hansom cab approaches and to the left of that you can see a cart carrying a milk churn. Until recently most of London's milk had been supplied by herds of cows kept in sheds. By the time of this painting 'railway milk' was brought in by trains from the countryside.

The State of the River Thames

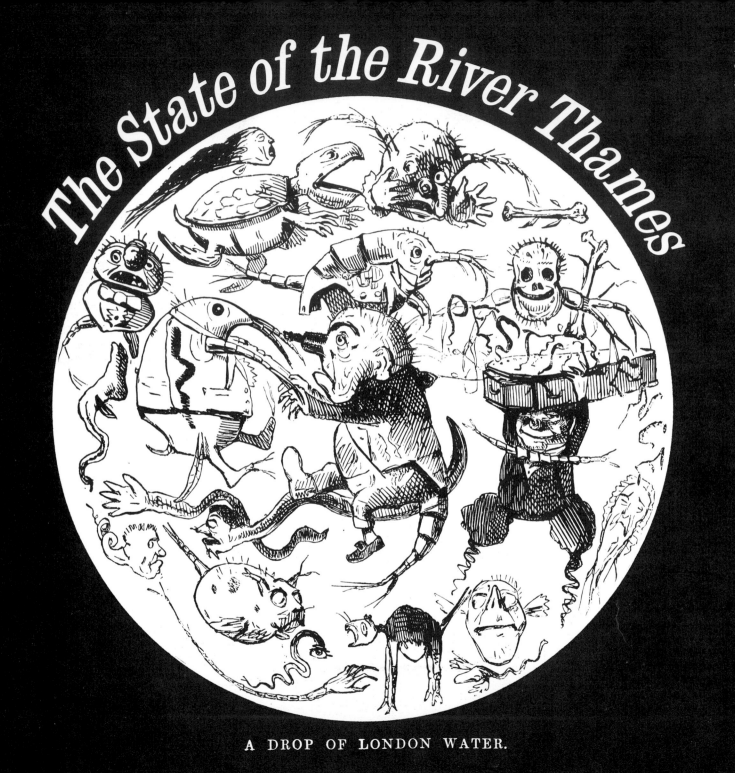

A DROP OF LONDON WATER.

If some artists avoided the subject of dirt and disease, the cartoonists were quite prepared to draw attention to London's problems. In particular they concentrated on showing how polluted London's water had become.

By the middle of the 19th century the population of London had reached over 2 million. This number of people produced a lot of waste and a great deal of sewage. Yet there was no real system for getting rid of it. Most of it found its way into the Thames, where it floated backwards and forwards on the tide. The smell that rose up from the mud-banks at low tide was particularly awful. In 1858 it was so bad that the Members of Parliament had to abandon their discussions and people crossing the bridges felt sick. This was named 'The Year of the Great Stink'.

London also had a very limited water supply. It was not unusual for many households to have to use a single pump or tap.

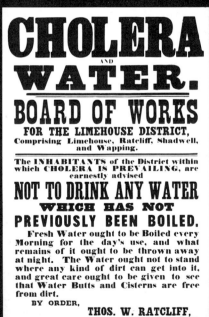

CHOLERA
AND
WATER.
BOARD OF WORKS
FOR THE LIMEHOUSE DISTRICT,
Comprising Limehouse, Ratcliff, Shadwell,
and Wapping.

The INHABITANTS of the District within which CHOLERA IS PREVAILING, are earnestly advised

NOT TO DRINK ANY WATER
WHICH HAS NOT
PREVIOUSLY BEEN BOILED.

Fresh Water ought to be Boiled every Morning for the day's use, and what remains of it ought to be thrown away at night. The Water ought not to stand where any kind of dirt can get into it, and great care ought to be given to see that Water Butts and Cisterns are free from dirt.

BY ORDER,

THOS. W. RATCLIFF,
CLERK OF THE BOARD.

Board Offices, White Horse Street,
1st August, 1866.

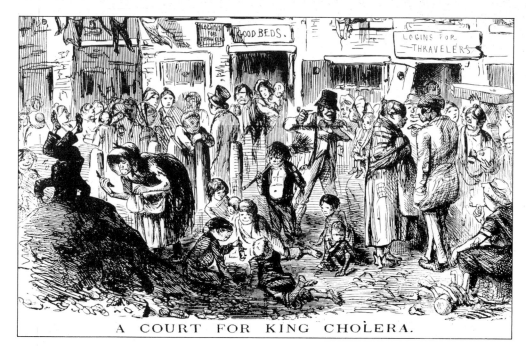

A COURT FOR KING CHOLERA.

THE "SILENT HIGHWAY" - MAN.
"Your MONEY or your LIFE!"

Sometimes leaking sewage polluted the water and this led to outbreaks of a fearful disease called cholera which killed hundreds of people. In the middle of the 19th century London was in danger of poisoning itself.

The problem was summed up by a letter in *The Times* newspaper from a group of people living in the slum area of St Giles. Their spelling wasn't very good but they did have a point to make.

'Sur, may we beg and beseech your proteckshion and power . . . we live in muck and filthe. We aint got no privy, no dust bins, no drains, no water supplies . . . if the Colera comes Lord help us . . .'

Conditions in St Giles were very bad indeed. It was estimated that 3,000 people lived in less than one hundred houses. Many families could only afford the rent of a single room. Very often they might sub-let part of the room to those poorer than themselves. The result was terrible overcrowding.

The illustrations above give a good idea of the conditions in which many people lived. Only a few houses had water closets. Some had a simple wooden lavatory seat. Sewage would drop into a cess-pit. If this was not regularly emptied by the night-soil men, it would overflow and endanger any nearby water supplies. As you can see an open sewer is flowing under this house. Why did people put up with these conditions? By and large because they had no alternative.

Solving London's many problems was not easy because there was no central authority prepared to take charge. In 1855 the Government set up the Metropolitan Board of Works and things began to improve. The chief engineer was a man called Joseph Bazalgette. He constructed an embankment along the northern edge of the Thames from Westminster to Blackfriars. This involved building a massive wall in the river and then infilling with huge amounts of soil. Buried under the Embankment was an 8-foot (2.5m) wide pipe which caught most of the city's sewage and took it well down river before allowing it to flow out into the Thames. The construction of a drainage system for London was one of the great achievements of the Victorian engineers. Other pipes carried gas, water and telegraph wires. Further away from the river ran what was to be a section of London's underground railway system. The underground railway had many opponents. *The Times* said

'*. . . it is an insult to common sense to suppose that people . . . would ever prefer . . . to be driven amid palpable darkness through the foul subsoil of London.*' *The Times* was wrong. The underground, or 'Drain' as it was called, was an instant success.

On the top of the embankment a new spacious road was laid out. This greatly relieved the traffic jams in the Strand. In the area reclaimed from the Thames, gardens were laid out and some fine new buildings constructed.

This painting was made in the 1860s just as work on the Victoria Embankment was coming to an end. If you look on the extreme right you will see work still in progress. Of course the Embankment could not continue any further south because the new Palace of Westminster blocked the way. It too had been built out into the river.

The first Palace of Westminster was built by Edward the Confessor in the 11th century. It was constructed on land that lay between his Abbey and the Thames. You can just see the twin towers of Westminster Abbey in the distance. Today the Palace of Westminster refers to the building containing the Houses of Parliament: the House of Commons and the House of Lords.

The House of Commons continued to meet in St Stephen's Chapel until 1834 when it was destroyed in a huge fire. The new *Houses of Parliament* were built in a medieval style to match the Abbey.

In the painting you can see the clock tower. This is now usually called *Big Ben* although originally the name referred only to the largest bell. At the time of the painting the huge clock faces were illuminated by sixty gas jets.

Behind the clock tower stand the Houses of Parliament themselves dominated by the *Victoria Tower* 336 feet (102 m) high. In this building laws were made which affected people throughout Britain's huge overseas Empire.

51

◀ Tower Bridge was opened by the Prince of Wales in 1894. It was a great occasion as you can see from the painting on the opposite page. The river was crowded with steamers and there were flags everywhere. The bridge was needed to ease the traffic jams on London Bridge.

The bridge was an extraordinary piece of engineering. It was as extra-ordinary in its day as the *Thames Barrier* is for us. The roadway which runs across the bridge can be lifted in two huge sections like a double drawbridge. This is to allow tall ships to pass into the Pool of London. These sections are called bascules. Each bascule weighs 1,000 tons (1016 tonnes). Originally the job of raising the bascules was done by steam-driven machinery. Today electricity is used.

So that people on foot were not delayed when the bridge was up, a high level walkway was constructed 142 feet (43.28 m) above the river. This was reached by lifts and stairways in the towers. The towers themselves were designed to look like medieval castles with narrow windows and clusters of pinnacles sitting on top. This was done so that the bridge should remain in keeping with the Tower of London nearby. Although Tower Bridge pretends to look older than it really is, it does provide London with a dramatic gateway. The silhouette of Tower Bridge is known throughout the world as a symbol of London.

Today if you go to visit the Tower of London don't forget to have a look at Tower Bridge. You can walk across the walkway and enjoy marvellous views up and down the river. You can also examine the machinery which operates the bascules.

The River Thames and dockland looking East ▶

You can see Tower Bridge on the bottom edge of this aerial view. This painting shows the river Thames flowing out towards the North Sea. You can see the docks built early in the 19th century. As ships got bigger so the problems of sailing all the way up the Thames got greater and greater. The docks were originally built for sailing ships and there was also the problem of enlarging these so that steamers could use them. In recent years new docks have been constructed at *Tilbury* much closer to the mouth of the Thames. Today much of the old dockland lies empty and derelict. But plans exist to redevelop this area by building new houses where once ships used to unload. The docks themselves may be turned into yachting marinas or leisure centres. This is what happened to St Katharine's Dock which lies close to the Tower (see page 4). Look at this painting and see if you can see the West India Docks which was described on page 39.

The Age of the Motor Car

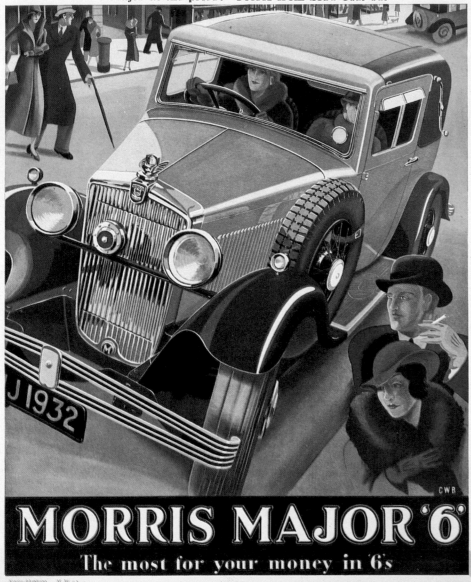

The first cars appeared in London streets at the beginning of the 20th century during the reign of King Edward VII. However, these early cars were enormously expensive. It was not until the 1930s that popular motoring started as mass-produced cars began to appear in huge numbers. Since then the problem of the motor car has been one of London's biggest headaches. Cars are certainly very convenient but they do clog up narrow streets, car exhaust is bad for your health and each year many car accidents cause injury and death.

London's first motor-buses appeared on the streets in 1899. To start with they were dirty and noisy and frequently broke down. By 1912 they were greatly improved and enormously popular with the public. Buses with covered top decks did not appear until 1925. The word 'General' stood for London General Omnibus Company. In 1933 the London Transport Board was set up to control bus and underground services. The motor-bus killed off the horse-drawn bus fairly quickly. Horses were still used to pull carts for another forty years and only finally disappeared after the Second World War.

Advert for Underground ▶

London was continuing to grow. Many people who worked in central London could now decide to live 5 or 6 miles away in one of the new, leafy suburbs like *Golders Green*. Here spacious detached and semi-detached houses were being built for well-to-do people. A garden and a short walk to the station were other advantages of moving to the outer suburbs. Of course people now had to spend longer travelling to work. It would take at least forty-five minutes for this man to reach his office in the City. Many people who bought houses in the country soon found themselves surrounded by new houses as the suburbs continued to develop.

Fleet Street in 1930 ▶ ▶

What would Christopher Wren have made of this view of his great Cathedral? Compare this painting with the engraving made by Gustave Doré only 60 years earlier from a similar viewpoint. The artist called his painting 'Amongst the nerves of the World'. Can you explain this title? Do you remember why Fleet Street is important?

UNDERGROUND

THE SOONEST REACHED AT ANY TIME

GOLDERS GREEN
(HENDON AND FINCHLEY)

LONDON AT WAR

Twice in the 20th century the citizens of London have found themselves involved in a World War.

The First World War was fought far away, but in the Second World War London found itself in the front line. From September 1940 until May 1941, wave after wave of German bombers came droning through the night.

The main targets were the docks, warehouses and railway stations in the East End of London. Inevitably many of the bombs fell in among the closely packed streets causing terrible damage and loss of life. In one night alone 1436 people were killed. By the end of the war 100,000 homes had been destroyed and a million more needed to be repaired.

Many of London's famous buildings were damaged; the Tower of London, Westminster Abbey and Buckingham Palace were all hit by bombs. In a single night ten of the beautiful churches designed by Wren were burnt out. But it was St Paul's Cathedral that people were most concerned about. One Londoner is reported as saying '*You know, mate, I ain't a religious bloke. I never go to church and I don't pray or anything. But I should hate to see old St Paul's hurt or*

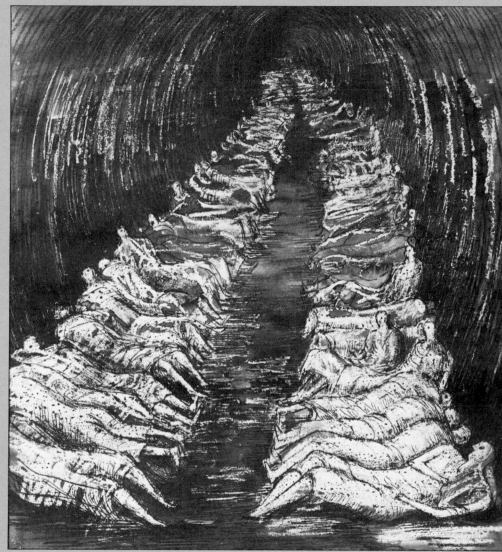

damaged. Somehow, you know, it's London, ain't it?'

On the left you can see what is perhaps the most famous photograph of London taken during the war. It shows St Paul's in London surrounded by smoke and flames but still surviving.

At the height of each attack the fire fighters fought the flames. The rescue workers dug among the rubble of collapsed buildings for people who had been buried. Ambulance drivers took the injured to hospital through the blocked and dangerous streets. Other people

sheltered where they could.

Some would spend the night in the shelters they had built in their backgardens. Others went to the public shelters or down into the underground stations. It wasn't much fun but eventually people got used to it.

The drawing above was made by an artist called Henry Moore. His pictures are not realistic like a photograph but they give a strong sense of what it must have been like in these deep underground tunnels while so much terror was raging up above.

The Blitz. That is the name people gave to the air-raids on the cities during the Second World War. It is from a German word '*blitzkrieg*' meaning lightning war.

The people of London took a great deal of trouble to blackout their houses. They fixed up heavy blinds or curtains so that no chink of light could escape and help the enemy bombers find their targets. The street lights were turned off and cars were driven with only their side lights on. People hated the dark and many accidents happened. When the air-raids finally came, the bombers dropped incendiaries which started huge fires lighting up the sky for miles around.

The large painting on this page was made by an artist called L. Rosoman. In it you can see a building in Cheapside well ablaze. Rosoman was a fireman. Every night he and his colleagues struggled to save London from the flames while around them the air-raids went on. In the other picture you can see a group of firemen on a roof-top near St Paul's.

This picture was painted by Graham Sutherland. He was an official war artist and he had the job of recording an impression of some of the damage caused by the air-raids. Here he shows us a bombed-out street in the East End of London. These houses were once the homes of many families. Now they stand silent and empty.

This is what Graham Sutherland said about his painting: '*In the City one didn't think of the destruction of life. All the destroyed buildings were office buildings and people weren't in them at night. But in the East End one did think of the hurt to people. . . . Even a mattress that had been blown out of a house into the street looked more like a body. . . . the shell of long terraces of* houses . . . *great – surprisingly wide – perspectives of destruction seeming to recede into infinity, the windowless blocks were like sightless eyes.*'

Despite all their suffering during the war the people of London grumbled and carried on with their lives as best they could. '*We can take it,*' was a slogan you often heard. '*Business as usual.*'

59

London since the war...

In May 1945, the war finally came to an end. The blackout rules were lifted. The street-lights were turned on and very slowly life got back to normal. It took many years to repair the damage war had caused and even longer to cope with some of the problems the war had revealed, such as the poor conditions in which many people lived.

Since the war there have been big improvements in housing. Although mistakes were made in building too many high-rise blocks in which people could feel lonely and cut off from their neighbours, housing schemes today are generally more carefully designed.

London air is much cleaner since smoky coal fires were banned. Now people worry about the effect of lead pollution caused by car exhausts.

Cars and traffic remain one of London's biggest problems despite the fact that many new roads and underpasses have been built.

Since the war London has stopped growing. In fact, the population is now declining. The 'green belt', a strip of countryside surrounding London on which it is forbidden to build, has stopped London spreading ever outwards.

London Transport has struggled with the problem of keeping London on the move and, by and large, has been successful. Tube trains now run out to Heathrow, the busiest airport in the world.

At Woolwich the Thames Barrier is complete. This is an extraordinary series of specially designed steel gates set in the river bed which will protect London from flooding when tides are exceptionally high.

Running a city in which nearly seven million people live is no easy task. Everybody has their own view about the way things should be done. Perhaps the biggest problem in the mid 1980s is deciding how London shall be governed. How will the money be raised for providing all the things that Londoners need and want?

How should this money be spent? There will be a lot of discussion about this subject in the future. So keep your eye on the news.

The Barbican ▶

On the page opposite you can see our artist's impression of the *Barbican*, one of the most interesting developments to be built in the City since the war. It lies to the north of St Paul's just beyond the City Wall.

After the war it was said that the only people who lived in the City were caretakers and cats. So one of the ideas behind the Barbican was to encourage people to live in the heart of London again. Today there are enough flats here for 6,500 people. There are also shops, pubs and restaurants and a fine new arts centre. The church in the centre of the picture is St Giles, Cripplegate which was built in the 1500s. See if you can find it on the map on page 11.

People's views about the Barbican differ. Some think it a cold, unfriendly, concrete jungle. Others think that with its lakes and walk-ways and soaring towers it is a fine example of modern architecture. You must judge for yourself.

You may well go to the Barbican when you visit London because in the south-west corner overlooking a section of the original wall stands the Museum of London. This is a marvellous place. The galleries and exhibitions illustrate in great detail the history of London from the earliest times to the present day. If this book has made you curious about the history of London, then the Museum of London is one place you really ought to visit.

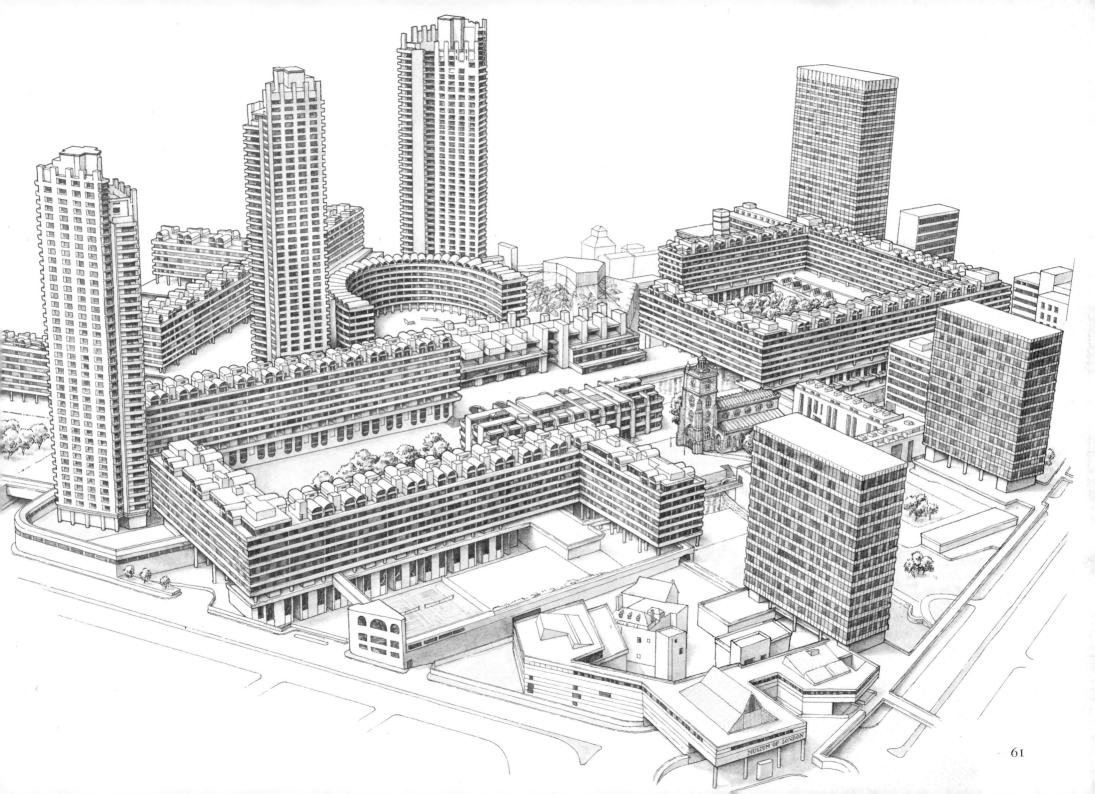

MUSEUM OF LONDON

To end our book we asked our photographer to take a photograph of London from a viewpoint similar to some of the paintings and illustrations you have seen in this book. The photograph was taken from an office block just to the south of London Bridge. Here you can see the sweep of the city from St Paul's in the west on the left to the Tower in the east on the right. Notice that the camera has distorted the river. It does not bend as the photograph suggests.

Immediately in front of us is the new London Bridge. It was only completed in 1973. It has room for six lanes of traffic and wide pavements for all the pedestrians who use it each day. Underground heating cables keep both road and pavement free from ice and snow. Notice that this bridge only has three spans compared with the twenty-one arches of the medieval bridge built by Peter de Colechurch. Of course in his day the river was much wider than it is now.

Notice how empty the river Thames has become. Why do you think this is? The great majority of boats using the river are pleasure craft carrying tourists. You may think that much of the old excitement and bustle has gone. But so also has most of the dirt and disease and poverty of earlier times. Even the river Thames itself is much cleaner today than for many years. Salmon have begun to return. However, some Londoners think that more use could be made of the river.

St Paul's Cathedral

Barbican Towers

National Westminster Tower

The Monument

London Bridge

If you look closely you will see a gap in the buildings on the river bank just downstream of London Bridge. This is Billingsgate. Soon a modern office block will be constructed here. Archaeologists working on this site have made a whole series of discoveries about how this area has been used in the past. Among other things, they have found massive timbers used by the Romans to build their waterfront, remains of a medieval church and traces of the Great Fire.

In the foreground on the right you can see some old buildings being demolished. Most of them are warehouses left over from the time when ships used to bring goods right into the heart of London. What should replace them? A park which is open for everybody to enjoy the view? Shops and restaurants for tourists? Office blocks which will provide jobs for many people? Private housing for the very wealthy? Perhaps a combination of all these ideas?

On this page you can see what London looked like on a bright, spring day in April 1984. Compare this picture with that on pages 16–19 showing what London looked like during the reign of the first Queen Elizabeth. By the time you read this, the photograph will be out of date. Something will have changed. A new building may have been constructed. An old building may have been demolished. What has happened in London since April 1984? What do you think will happen next?

Custom House

Tower of London

HMS Belfast

Bovis

Billingsgate

INDEX

Page numbers printed in **bold face** refer to pictures or maps.

© British Broadcasting Corporation 1984
First published 1984. Reprinted 1985, 1987
Published at the request of the School Broadcasting
Council for the United Kingdom by
BBC Books, a division of BBC Enterprises Limited,
Woodlands, 80 Wood Lane, London W12 0TT
Printed in England by Jolly & Barber Ltd, Rugby

Paperback   ISBN: 0 563 32703 0
Hardback   ISBN: 0 563 21358 2